I0810956

"Architecture comes from the making of a room."
_ Louis I. Kahn

Humbly, I would add

"And that room is empty."

THE EM TY ROOM

FRAGMENTED THOUGHTS ON SPACE

TABLE OF CONTENTS

PROLOGUE: A ROOM TO BEGIN WITH

We are accustomed to images/forms, and visual bombardment has already caused us to forget the meaning of these images and forms — consuming them as commodities; the form can recover its meaning when it faces darkness; in the darkness, through other qualities we arrive at an image based on our own experience and imagination.

Abbas Kiarostami

A ROOM TO BEGIN WITH

Today architecture has turned into a mere media device at the service of external forces, opportunistically ephemeral and conveniently obscured. On the one hand, architectural productions are exhausted beyond reproach, and on the other hand, the consistent transmutation of architecture into an over-formalized institution has dragged the discipline towards its decadence. Architecture has come short to be a discipline and instead converted to be an industry, a part of commercial establishment. Accordingly, it has given up its capacity to offer a contribution to the world and has been reduced to be a service.

We are living in an era of distraction that is characterized by constantly changing trends, over-consuming images and products. We are lacking the desire to focus and concentrate, missing the patience to wait, rushing to take shortcuts at any price in order to achieve success and draw attention; and of course, let us not forget that we have always known how to justify our desires — novelty in particular.

Obsessed with the visible and the tangible, and always lacking time, we are falling into an era in which we do not get a chance to focus, search, investigate, explore, or delve deeply. We are happy with the veneer, the facade, the mask, the surface and the very exterior of every phenomenon.

We might be living in the age of information, when all sorts of data are available to everyone in infinite quantities and fast speed. But we have to remember that knowledge and wisdom are different. Owning the former will not necessarily guarantee possessing the latter. While knowledge is the accumulation of data, like a large supermarket with tons of choices on the shelves for us to select and shop, one could define wisdom as a collection of experiences layered through the course of history, which is marinated with strategic abilities to process and create. Unfortunately, life has become about shopping through a catalogue rather than about inventing a path.

When it comes to architecture, it has become all about novelty. Architecture is practiced as a form-making exercise, in which one creates a form and dresses it up with a fashionable skin. What matters most is the look of it, and the contest to keep that look relevant in the media, as long as possible. It submits itself to a sick competition for visibility. The more awe it creates, the more viral it becomes. What used to be an autonomous discipline and a source of inspiration, stimulation, and motivation, now has become the subject of entertainment, speculation, and show business.

Now, it is necessary, or rather urgent, to pause, take a moment, go inward, search for the essentials, and hope to rediscover a principle which is at once basic, even generic, and timeless.

Where to begin then?

Well, as Kahn says: “Architecture comes from the making of a room”. So, let us start with this, the very desire to dwell in a space in its most basic form — a room.

The Empty Room

When we think about space, we have only looked at its enclosures. As if space itself is invisible, all theory for production of space is based on an obsessive preoccupation with its opposite: substance and objects, i.e. architecture. Architects could never explain space; Junkspace is our punishment for their mystifications.

Rem Koolhaas

THE EMPTY ROOM

Today more than ever,
I feel that cell No. 461
has remained inside me,
becoming the secret of my
soul. Today more than ever,
I feel like a bird that has
swallowed his cage. I take
my cell with me, inside me,
as a pregnant woman carries
her baby in her womb.

Curzio Malaparte

THE EMPTY ROOM

Once, I closed my eyes. I cannot recall whether I was asleep, had just blinked, or was trapped in a dreamworld. But when I opened my eyes, the only thing I could remember was a room though not an ordinary one. The room was completely empty, full of voidness. So, I called it the empty room.

The empty room was slightly higher than the ground, so when entering the room, one could feel that one's soul was being detached from the world. The empty room was neither too large nor too small. It was just the right size. After all, the right scale is much more important than largeness or smallness. Indeed, its true value came from being just, not more or less.

For instance, I could unroll my Gabbeh in the empty room, and there was still enough space left around it. Neither the room suffocated the Gabbeh, nor did the Gabbeh make the room look smaller or larger.

While full of voidness, the empty room was not empty. It was filled with memories, some of which have not even been realized yet. Temptations and desires were overflowing. The empty room was pregnant. The empty room did not welcome extreme heat or harsh cold. It had thick walls, so thick that one could hide inside it. The empty room was full of loneliness, but it was not lonely.

Once, inside the empty room, there was a tree. Another time, it was a reflection pool. And there was still enough space left, so that one could walk around the tree and the water, and sometimes lean back on the wall to throw one's feet into the puddle. Part of the empty room was always open to the sky, as if heaven was part of its ceiling. The tree could touch the sun. The water could hold the moon in its hand, alone or together with the stars. Sometimes, it kissed the rain. One could light a fire, stare at the sky and remember that one could always dream. One's soul grew in the empty room along with one's hopes.

During the day, the light came in through this oculus. The empty room made love with the light, and together they gave birth to shadows, which like vivid children, couldn't stay still.

The empty room didn't have an outside, or the exterior formal shape was not its concern at all. Indeed, the empty room had come to existence to define the inside. Otherwise, the outside has always been there.

The empty room was not intended for an ordinary life. Life in its routine definition could spoil the empty room's capacity. The empty room was for falling in love, reading fables, contemplating, praying, singing, crying, and above all reminding one of being human.

Since this empty room has occupied my mind, all the other rooms with different adjectives became unattractive to me, and have lost their tenancy: the long room, the narrow room, the large room, the high room, the wide room, the chic room, the luxury room, and, interestingly, the beautiful room as well.

Among all rooms, I liked the empty room the most. It was a room that was no longer in the world, but the whole world was in the empty room.

We all have this empty room with us. We project our very soul in this room. Our room will become us, and we will become our rooms. Before we know, we have become one with our room. Our room is always empty, it is weightless, but its charged with thoughts, memories, and emotions. It is an inventory, and its beauty lies in the fact that its capacity is indefinite.

Most of the times we refuse to acknowledge this room; often we lose it, and what a pity it is that every now and then, we rent it! Not to mention that by mistake or by force, we may also dwell in wrong rooms, occasionally in rooms that do not deserve us or those that we do not deserve. Our room fits our soul.
It grows and declines with us.

We take this room everywhere all the time. We measure every space/place with our very own room. Thats how we find different spaces large, small, narrow, tall, short, dark, cozy, intimidating, and the like. Every time we enter a space, it is our room that affects our judgment and perception. Any place that is in tune with our room comforts us.

As we grow, our room will grow with us. We change, and our room will adapt. Our room is always a more or less a distinct definition of space according to our way of living and of understanding of the surrounding environment, a very elaborate combination of our physical experiences and mental perceptions.

When we interact with each other, we open our rooms to each other. We invite each other to our rooms. Some of us have rooms with no openings. Some have rooms as pavilions, always open and welcoming. Some make their rooms their fortresses of solitudes. When you love someone, the empty room becomes smaller, more intimate, for it encourages you to hug, to become one with your lover. Sometimes, if you listen well to your room, it tells you who is welcome and who is not.

One should take good care of this empty room. If we by ignorance gradually let in jealousy, sadness, anger, and greed into it, then we loose our desire to take refuge in our empty room. We will forget it, and will lose it. Without the empty room, we are restless and anxious, for no room is even close to our own empty room. We should purge it often, and let our empty room breathe fresh air.

...

All the great masterpieces of architecture embrace this empty room in one way or another. Architecture is to create this empty room. It is to create the empty, not the room!

The Empty Room

One room! That makes a fantastic building. The most beautiful buildings have one room. But that room has to be ambitious.

Peter Zumthor

FRAGMENTED THOUGHTS ON SPACE

Beauty is the mystery of life. It is not in the eye, it is in my mind.

Agnes Martin

(1)

The empty room is always part of a larger system.
It is collective, yet alone, but not lonely.
We can be in the empty room in any room, in any building, in any place.

The empty room has its own identity.
It is defined or characterized innately.
We recognize its presence, which however, is often beyond descriptions or even consciousness.

The empty room is empty.
It is available to become, to host, to accept, and to offer.
We create freely and infinitely in the empty room, and it also actively participates.

The empty room is just.
It is measured and scaled morally enough.
We sense the empty room neither too large nor too small.

The empty room suggests opportunities every moment.
It is optimistic and full of hopes.
We seek to improve in the empty room, as it also does in us.

We work the clay in the shape of a vase, for it is precisely where there is nothing that the effectiveness of the vase resides. We make openings for doors and windows to make a house, for it is precisely where there is nothing that the effectiveness of the house resides.

Lao Tzu

(2)

The empty room has unmeasurable qualities.

The more we add to its measurability, the more the room becomes more ordinary. In adding each element, it loses its capacity to offer indefinite possibilities. It is in its most empty state that it offers its maximum capacity.

The empty room has unmeasurable qualities.

We can only measure it with our emotions, feelings, moods, and the like. It is exactly because of this fact we each perceive a spatial quality differently.

We find the very same room welcoming or intimidating under different circumstances; it becomes larger or smaller with different people.

The empty room has unmeasurable qualities.

We can give to or take from it, and gradually it becomes the room we want. It becomes our very extension.

The empty room is unmeasurable.

When there is less, we appreciate everything much more.

John Maeda

(3)

The empty room is a refuge — for mind.

The empty room is a shelter — for body.

The empty room is a sanctuary — for soul.

The emptier the room is, the more sensitive and responsive it becomes. It is a mirror for our soul. It listens to us carefully and reflects our feelings and thoughts back to us. It enters into a dialogue with us. We hear its voice, and of course, there is no noise or clutter in the empty room.

A profound architectural (spatial) experience is always an exchange; I enter the space and the space enters me, I leave part of myself in the building and the building becomes part of my self-image, travelling with me forever.

Juhani Pallasmaa

(4)

Every time we enter the empty room, we discover and rediscover how to inhabit the space.

The empty room is heuristic. It stimulates and enables possibilities. We learn and discover new usage each and every day and everyday.

The empty room exists prior to specific need. Unrestricted by any contingencies, it is always another place.

The empty room is not a place without purpose. It exceeds all purposes. It is capable of embracing all of us who have specific desires.

The empty room does not have a name. It suggests itself and its use. That comes from the way we discover it. It is personal and private to each and every one of us.

The empty room is incomplete and accidental. It lends itself to be completed with our presence, and to be contingent as a result of our acts.

The empty room asks for its release to its original freedom, to its emptiness. Think of ruins: they are discharged from their original purpose and are now free to become. In order to offer, they become empty rooms again.

The difference between a good and poor architect is that the poor architect succumbs to every temptation and the good one resists it.

Ludwig Wittgenstein

(5)

Every time we enter the empty room, the space becomes smaller and more intense. Our body subtracts the space, and our soul fills its air. The emptiness of the room becomes sad, happy, discouraged, or inspired, accordingly.

When one leaves the empty room, an imprint of our body remains in the space. The space stays charged for a while in our absence. As if living, it remembers who was there.

The empty room expands and shrinks. It breathes like a lung, and the space is the air.

The empty room is sometimes divided into smaller empty rooms, by us, by light, by raising a wall, by time ...

In the fusion of place and soul, the soul is as much a container of place as a place is a container of soul.

Robert Pogue Harrison

(6)

The empty room is the emergence of architecture.

Architecture is to create, define, shape, support, and offer spatial experience. Space is the essence.

Gathering around the fire, we form the empty room. The intensity of the fire defines its size.

Sometimes, we seek a room, but the room is there already. A shaded area under a tree is an empty room which moves with the sun and hides with the night.

We also build a room ourselves, which we have been doing from the very beginning of our history. It was our primordial need and desire to dwell. And this very desire made the very first empty room.

The empty room is the beginning of architecture.
It is also its finale.

The room is the beginning of architecture. So sensitive is a room. It is the place of the mind.

Louis I. Kahn

(7)

Inside the empty room, the space feels dense. It stands anchored in gravity. It lingers in a pause, a moment. And it places us at the very centre of this tension. This happens regardless of its enclosure.

At the same time, the empty room becomes a second layer of skin for our body. It connects us to a larger place, even to the universe.

A profound empty room (the empty room is already profound) takes away our sense of continuum, and leads us into the quantum world, while it may simultaneously provide, even facilitate, our visual and physical connection to the outside.

It is the very emptiness of the empty room that pulls the space/place together. An enclosure may be capable of containing conditions (to contain the temperature, and the like), but the sense of roominess is something different. We can impose a spatiality with an enclosure, but the empty room never forces but only invites, offers, suggests, and, sometimes, tempts.

The empty room cherishes the contained, not the container, the space, not the enclosure.

Empty your mind,
be formless, shapeless,
like water.

Bruce Lee

(8)

The empty room earnestly offers earnest possibilities so that we can identify with it. Of course, we must also empty our mind and free it from all preoccupations, to receive what the empty room has to offer. The freer our mind is, the more possibilities the empty room can offer.

Then, the empty room will become a place to dwell for us, a shelter for our body, a refuge for our mind, a sanctuary for our soul. It will empower us to think, imagine, dream and as Heidegger says,
"to poetically dwell."

The empty room does not attend to us as we are, but as we desire ourselves to be. Likewise, if we are preoccupied with the mere image of a chair next to a window, this is what we will get; this will become the only offering.

The empty room wants to offer infinite possibilities; it always waits for us to receive all its goodness.

If men truly lived as men,
their houses would be temples.

Mario Botta

(9)

The empty room does not force an attention to itself. It invites us to choose to see the qualities of its setting, its place, and its locale.

The empty room does not dictate a fixed way of inhabiting. Yet, it suggests and offers possibilities, and accepts and encourages particularities.

The empty room locates us and becomes a stopping place for us, where our mind can rest, and our soul can sleep. It inspires us to live our vocation, not to be a tourist of the ephemeral (globalization, consumerism, materialism, digital media, and speed).

While we are gradually losing our capacity to take a moment and reflect, and to dwell in space and time, the empty room offers a place of repose, where time is stretched in space. This is a thick time of an eternal nature, not a thin one of a secular property.

Only by keeping silent does one encounter the moment. When one speaks, even if one says only a single word, one misses the moment. Only in silence is the moment. Beginning is the art of becoming silent.

Kierkegaard

(10)

The empty room is empty so that we can project our personality into it. There is no way to completely represent the empty room, for it only exists in our perception. We understand it by our very own subjective means. Thus, we must not attempt to search for words to define it, or tools to draw the empty room. Instead we must search for a way to feel it, and to be immersed in it. Through spatial experiences, we attain an awareness of its very existence, its very emptiness.

The empty room acquires its profound character by creating a field of relationships, a setting ready to become. This is beyond borrowing a definition by means of an enclosure. The true definition comes from the inside (space), not from the outside (envelope).

The empty room is a place of possibilities, where the physical, the mental, and the spiritual keep merging into each other.

I am the space, where I am.

Noel Arnaud

(11)

The empty room leads us to confront our very existence in utmost sensitivity, consciousness, and truthfulness.

We can grasp the empty room when we dedicate our whole being. Simply seeing in a physical sense (boundaries, containers, and enclosures) can only give us shallow hints about the empty room.

Imagine a cup of tea: the cup shapes a visual boundary of the tea, which, nonetheless, is formless by nature. To understand the tea itself, we should hold the cup, feel its weight and warmth, smell the aroma, have a first sip, taste the texture, put the cup down, reflect on the experience, and prepare in mind and body to repeat this once more.

In the empty room, it is in the emptiness itself where the true effectiveness resides.

We think we benefit from things that are tangible, but it is precisely where we do not perceive anything that true effectiveness resides.

Lao Tzu

(12)

The empty room renews our memories and spurs our imagination. It is the setting in which we capture a moment between the past and the future. The empty room motivates us to think, recall, and imagine, and then it fades into a pixel within an entire image that has inspired us.

We record the empty room, and the empty room records us. The empty room is stored in our body, mind, and soul, and it returns to us again and again as a recollection. At the same time, the empty room is a memory device itself. It amplifies, evokes, or rejects a recollection; it exalts or despairs a sensation.

The empty room does not originate anything. It only reframes our own emotions and thoughts, and hands them back to us.

The empty room is a mirror for our soul.

We are what we remember.

Juhani Pallasma

(13)

The empty room suggests slowness.

There is a secret bond between slowness and memory, between speed and forgetting.

Milan Kundera

(14)

The empty room is empty in order to have a chance to become our room. We release our mind in the empty room where it is received, processed, and sent back to us.

Think of Ise Shrine: it has been completely dismantled and reassembled once every twenty years exactly in the same way for 1,300 years. Yet, the empty room has always been intact, continuously. It has nothing to do with building a structure. The empty room has always already been there.

My Father's house has many rooms; if that were not so, would I have told you that I am going there to prepare a place for you?

John 14:2

(15)

The empty room offers the space. It becomes the place with us. It adjusts itself not only to the measurable quantities of the room, but to the physiology and psychology of our body and mind, and to our spirituality.

The empty room is an experiential place, not a dead void. It is an entity with boundaries, sizes, and scales. Yet, the very same space becomes a different place for another person. The placeness of the empty room comes from our feelings, memories, images, and all other conceptions and perceptions which vary from person to person.

The empty room is subjective.

Space is in essence that for which room has been made, that which is let into its bounds.

Heidegger

(16)

The empty room is waiting like a womb to become pregnant. The space becomes the place as the empty room adapts itself to our very specificities, and we adapt ourselves to the spirit of the empty room. Its spirit is the very reflection of our soul — our desires, intentions, memories, and very inner worlds. The empty room becomes familiar with us, and we become familiar with the empty room.

Although the empty room becomes the place with us and for us, it does not mean that it is a non-place. It is in the constant state of becoming, being all the places and exceeding them at once.

The empty room is a necessary space. It grants us a capacity, a legible space for action and meditation. We become particular through the empty room, and the empty room becomes particular through us.

Nothing we do is unplaced.

Edward S. Casey

(17)

What defines reality in the empty room?

Not its dimensional, functional, stylistic, or technical matters on their own, but the intangible relation and bond between time, space/place, and memory.

The empty room merges all our perceptions into one. Our intellectual (geometric and tectonic qualities) and phenomenological (sensory and emotional qualities) understandings become indistinguishable and inseparable in it.

When you have not learned about lines, planes, and points, you are restricted to seeing only with your senses.

Sana'i

(18)

The empty room can only be understood through a spatial experience, by being present in it tactilely, visually, sensually, and emotionally. It cannot be reduced to bare information (construction specification), nor decoded to a flat representation (drawings).

This is exactly why it is hard, almost impossible, to capture the empty room with any visual means or to represent it with any drawings. We can only record the empty room in our memory.

But baby I've been here before; I've seen this room and I've walked this floor.

Leonard Cohen

(19)

The empty room is incomplete.

It only becomes complete through our imagination. We each reconstruct it as an ideal space/place in our own way.

The empty room is unfinished.

It suggests a possibility and contains a contingency so that we can take part. We contribute to it, barrow from it, or interact with it.

The empty room is participatory.

Architectural space can take away or awaken abilities and sensations that we possess innately.

Go Hasegawa

(20)

A form emerges, which can be unpredictable and imperceptible, whereas a figure has a past or a sort of connection, which therefore implies recognition.

The empty room directs us to an original source (a figure), in which to discover and remember an idea (a form).

Accordingly, it becomes our room in a very specific way that we discover (imagination) and we remember (memory).

The empty room materializes according to our imagination and memories. It is we, who by dwelling in it, extract an idea or form of the space/place.

Then the empty room becomes a room for each of us. It becomes our room.

Thought dwells in emptiness.

Kenya Hara

(21)

The empty room helps us understand and experience interiority. And it is with the interiority that exteriority becomes tangible. Interiority creates an inner space/place that according to Bachelard "... invites [our] mind to go on holiday for a while and think about nothing which means everything".

At this age of extreme connectivity, the empty room creates a moment of disconnect and isolation. Thus we can liberate ourselves from the ephemerality of our world and contemplate the meaningful, to break free from constant distraction and breathe and dream!

The empty room responds to our need for intimacy, our innate desire to be ourselves regardless of what is around. It is from dwelling in our very own self that we reemerge, restart, renew, recharge, and bring our imagination back to its purity.

Be a loner. That gives you time to wonder, to search for the truth. Have holy curiosity. Make your life worth living.

Albert Einstein

(22)

The empty room suggests/offers a journey to us.
By entering the empty room, we enter not simply into a room, but a part of our deep-rooted psyche.

In our domestic spaces, we bring together the far away and the long ago in order to create a private universe.

Walter Benjamin

(23)

In the end, each and every empty room becomes the collective memory of all the people who have dwelled in it, in the past, present, and future.

A cage went in search of a bird.

Franz Kafka

(24)

The emptiness of the empty room is different from a vacuum or nothingness. It is always articulated by and charged with something. It is intense.

The empty room may be empty, but its inertia is not equal to zero.

It is one thing to see with the eyes, another to see with the head.

Eduardo Souto de Moura

(25)

The empty room does not just hold the space but curates it.

Containers, envelopes, boundaries, and walls are just means of architecture. The end is the contained, the enveloped, and the invisible.

The empty room is not the space itself but the space curated.

To make a house, you grab a handful of air and you hold it together with a few walls.

Alberto Campo Baeza
(Nazarene Proverb)

(26)

The empty room waits for the sun all along the night, night after night, every night, so that they can make love again.

Together they give birth to shadows. The affair lasts only for a day. The obsession lives forever.

This is the ideal, to keep falling in love with the beloved, day after day, every day.

Light and shade are
the loudspeakers of this
architecture of truth,
tranquility and strength.
Nothing further could
add to it.

Le Corbusier

(27)

The space contained in the empty room is limitless no matter how small the room is. It is a bare canvas on which our mind can travel freely.

In this era of consumerism, we are constantly confused and distracted by many values and inputs. We can barely hold our attention to one subject for more than a few seconds. It is a luxury to be in the empty room, to breathe deeply again, concentrate, slow down, focus, and dream, escaping from the delirious contemporary life.

Of course to appreciate the empty room a certain act of will is required. The empty room is not for the slothful who take dwelling for granted.

All the rooms which appeal to our soul are those that gained their characters from the essential qualities of space, not the ephemeral ones that only temporarily exist (imagine a hotel room, a ship's cabin, or a monk's cell).

The empty room is more iconoclastic at first. With our personas, the empty room becomes affiliated, associated, and affected. With us, it gains specific spices and tastes.

Thus, the empty room is a picture frame. Of course, the affection between the framed and the frame is mutual yet different. The former brings a character, while the latter provides an exposure, a setting, a context, or a stage if you will.

We need our rooms to align us to desirable versions of ourselves and to keep alive the important, evanescent sides of us.

Alain De Botton

(28)

The emptiness of the empty room challenges our notion of completeness. It is already present in this very emptiness, but is simultaneously improved through the continual process of purging, cleaning, and polishing.

While all thing are inherently beautiful; refined beauty can only be achieved through a long journey dedicated to it, which enables the refined beauty to exist as one body with its surroundings. Imagine a piece of stone: polished to a degree that its surface mirrors everything around; it becomes invisible in favour of something beyond; it becomes one with nature.

Only great minds can afford a simple style.

Stendhal

(29)

The empty room listens to us if we speak with our heart.

We can listen to the empty room if we close our eyes and open our mind.

In the empty room, our mind becomes sharp. It flows with the universe. The empty room is a place of concentration. It is a place of vigilance where the mind sees the neglected truth and beauty.

Your desire is to see, then listen; hearing is a step towards vision.

St. Bernard of Clairvaux

(30)

We should experience the empty room by being in it. No empty room becomes complete on its own. The presence of a dweller is fundamental. This precedes the sensations.

A room is only as good as you feel when you are in it.

Philip Johnson

***

How do we describe the empty room?
How do we change our perception?
How do we see the invisible?
How do we present and communicate it to the world?

Oh, many are Indians and Turks that speak the same tongue; oh, many the pair of Turks that are as strangers. Therefore, the tongue of mutual understanding is different indeed; to be one in heart is better than to be one in tongue.

Rumi

POSTSCRIPT: NOTHING VS EVERYTHING

Oh you without knowledge, the corporeal shape is nothing. It can be supposed that what the world has not, is, and what it has, is not.

Omar Khayyam

NOTHING VS EVERYTHING*

We can barely find any definition that tries to describe architecture without dealing with the very concept of space. Yet, I believe there is no such a thing as space. Rather, space exists solely in our perception.
We understand it by our very own means. Therefore, we must not attempt to search for words to define space. Instead, we must search for a way to feel it through different spatial experiments. Then, through this process, we would gain an awareness of space.

It is the non-existence of space that elaborates our very perception of its existence and makes us aware of the surprising diversity of space. It is the concept of non-being instead of being which creates a more dominant and powerful sense of being than being itself. This is how we perceive music through silence, how we appreciate our beloved's presence during their absence, and how we understand space through voids, the emptiness.

Yet, emptiness does not mean nothingness or characterlessness. On the contrary, it is capable to represent indefinite conditions, a setting that is ready to be filled with proper content in a potential future. Here comes the imagination, the inventiveness of a creative mind. A mind that finds an empty space inspirational and significant and recognizes it as an in-between state, a waiting condition. An empty setting or a well-thought void possesses a chance to become a mies-en-scene by virtue of its receptive character.

It is very difficult to sustain the purity, the virginity, and the innocence of emptiness, because it can so easily be contaminated. The beauty comes from the constant temptation of invading the untouched territory.

I believe that is why architecture is all about — how to treat the emptiness. It is to construct a perception, to create a void, to respect the space and not fill it up.

If architecture manifests itself through a constant dynamic/dialogue between a container (enclosure) and a contained (space), then where does the real value exist? Considering this forceful tension between the two, which one is the cause and which one is the effect? And then, what is the architecture? Is it the cause or the result of this dynamic? Is it the container or the contained? Which one affects the other? Do we perceive a space to design an envelope, or do we design and build an enclosure to define a space? Which one is really the mold for the other? Which one originates the other?

Building an envelope with confining surfaces, fulfilling only pragmatic, functional, and tectonic requirements of an enclosure, often sabotages the spatial values. The container is so capable of absorbing the contained to its benefit. Architects should not let the container consume and spoil the contained, since it is the contained, the space, where the fundamental value of architecture is experienced. It has to be the contained, however invisible and intangible, which shapes the container. When one takes the reverse process, the result will not be a plastic work of arts, but just an artless and ingenuous effort to solve a tectonic problem.

Conventionally, it is the visible and tangible physical existence of a building that absorbs all the attention, and that is what we normally call "architecture". In this case, I would like to draw your attention to invisible voids, to "anti architecture".

SCHEMATIC CHART OF NOTHING VS EVERYTHING

PRIMACY OF SPACE

Void
Contained
Space
Mass of air
Volume
Sculpted
Scale
Conceptual
Exists between objects
Poetic
Mind sees (profound)
Visual
Multi-dimension
Stirs an emotion
Subtractive (confined in its outer limits)
Cave
Architecture (vocation / discipline)

PRIMACY OF STRUCTURE

Solid
Container
Enclosure
Envelope
Surface
Flat
Measure
Physical
Is the object itself
Tectonic
Eye sees (superficial)
Optical
Three-dimension
Realizes a building
Additive (aggregation of parts)
Nest
Construction (job / trend)

*
Aliabadi, Reza. "Void", rzlbdPOST Vol.02, Issue.02 Fall (2010).
Aliabadi, Reza. "RZLBD HOPSCOTCH: Seeking a territory for a vision", London: Artifice, 2017.

The Empty Room

Our bodies are given life from the midst of nothingness. Existing where there is nothing is the meaning of the phrase, 'form is emptiness'. That all things are provided for by nothingness is the meaning of the phrase, 'emptiness is form'. One should not think that these are two separate things.

Yamamato Tsunetomo

EPILOGUE

Man's deepest gazes are for empty space.

Paul Valéry

EPILOGUE

Looking back at my notebooks, I noticed that I had been collecting notes for this project since September 2016. It may seem a bit strange that I rely on writing records in notebooks (most of the time using Moleskin) and the fact that I am not comfortable typing directly on a word processor. First I have to write things down on a piece of paper and only then, for the sake of reproduction or representation, would I lend myself to transfer them into the digital media, not to mention that it is the same with thinking, designing and drawing. For inception, I cannot rely on the machine. Anyway, from the beginning, I always thought that I would rewrite a continuous text, and the finished work would be a rather long essay in a more formal format. However, in the meantime two incidents have deeply affected me and the outcome.

I read Walter Benjamin's *One-Way Street*. The book is composed of 60 short proses, in one of which he declares: "The work is the death mask of its conception". Far before we got into this fevered digital era, he had predicted very well that the traditional form of writing would not survive the capitalist world.

Another small book which was a big influence was Kafka's *Reflections on Sin, Hope, Suffering, and the True Way*. He compiled 109 aphorisms to capture the inception of his random thoughts on different topics. He believed that an aphorism in contrast to a distinct definition can appear to be abstract and metaphorical, and therefore empowers one to see beyond or to imagine instead of to picture!

Being fascinated by these two great works, their inspiring styles favouring the fragment over the finished work, and also by observing the zeitgeist of our time when we would rather flip images on our smartphones or tablets instead of reading a two-page long text, I have decided to present this small book in the form of a series of short passages. Eventually, the prologue and the epilogue became longer than all these snippets. One could open the printed work at any page and read a short text, which hopefully stimulates a thought to revisit the essence and the very idea of space and therefore architecture.

Also, despite the fact that I had some great precedents in mind to illustrate the theme and the concept of emptiness, I intentionally decided to avoid the inclusion of any images, so that one can imagine beyond preoccupations and visual references. However, a table/chart in the postscript is the only exception.

Last but not least, this old familiar theme could be said definitely in one page, possibly in a paragraph, or perhaps in only one sentence. Why, then, repeat similar thoughts over and over, and juxtapose them with many affirming quotes? Well, I guess, the point was to soak in and be saturated in this very idea of the empty room rather than just tasting it. After all to get drunk, you have to keep on drinking.

It is my hope that reading through these pages affects the way you perceive the space and hopefully allows you to look at architecture differently — most likely to see the invisible.

The Empty Room

Architecture is a habit of mind, not a profession.

Le Corbusier

ACKNOWLEDGEMENT

I have to start by thanking my long-time editor Ms. Ruth Grant. I am eternally grateful to her friendship, she was the first person who encouraged me to begin writing in English. This was in 2008 and all these years she has been a very good listener to my restless mind.

Next time we do T&T, espresso is on me :)

To my amazing brother Amir A. my companion on long road trips, who took the time out of his very busy academic schedule to proofread the text. His wisdom, keen insight, and good taste in music and science are priceless. There is a reason that he has a triple A — he knows what I am referring to.

I am looking for another road trip, so that we can continue with the rest of J. S. Bach's complete collection!

To Actar Publishers, who took a chance on a not very conventional concept and a not very easygoing author. I was very specific, having particular specs for the book — from its pocket size to its typography and its paper. They have been very accommodating.

Muchas gracias Ricardo por ser paciente con nosotros.

To everyone at Atelier RZLBD, who on a daily basis keep the ongoing discourse alive. A very special thanks to James Chungwon Park not only for asking intriguing questions all the time but also for reading the very first draft.

Kam-sa Ham-ni-da

Last but not least, to Harold Grabowski for always being the person I could turn to during all sort of challenging moments. Here's to you my Don.

Bowmore, no ice, just a drop of water.

Being obsessed with what I do, I can not deny that I have come short to give to my beloved ones. This humble book comes to life because of them.

I love you from my empty room.

RZLBD, Summer 2019

The Empty Room

AUTHOR'S BIOGRAPHY

Reza Aliabadi (RZLBD) is a Canadian architect of Persian origin. He is the founder of Atelier RZLBD, an art and architecture practice based in Toronto, whose work extends to crafting buildings, creating objects, making installations, and publishing a periodical zine called rzlbdPOST.

His work has been distinguished with numerous accolades including the International Architecture Master Prize (2018, 2019) American Architecture Prize (2017) and Ontario Association of Architects Awards (2009, 2011); exhibited in many venues including the Sir John Soane's Museum (London 2018) the World Architecture Festival (Berlin 2017, Amsterdam 2018) the School of Architecture at McGill University (Montreal 2009, 2017) and Toronto Harbourfront Centre (2012); and celebrated in more than one hundred print publications.

In 2017 RZLBD has been selected among the top emerging design talents in Canada. In the same year the UK publisher Artifice released a monograph, RZLBD HOPSCOTCH, which recognizes Reza's selected built projects by collecting essays, project profiles, and annotated drawings.

INVENTORY

Arnaud, Noel (1919 — 2003); French author.

Bachelard, Gaston (1884 — 1962); French philosopher.

Baeza, Alberto Campo (1946); Spanish architect.

Bernard of Clairvaux (1090 — 1153); French abbot.

Brodsky, Joseph (1940 — 1996); Russian-American Poet.

Botta, Mario (1943); Swiss architect.

Benjamin, Walter (1892 — 1940); German philosopher, cultural critic and essayist.

Casey, Edward S. (1939); American philosopher.

Chatwin, Bruce (1940 — 1989); English writer.

Cohen, Leonard (1934 — 2016); Canadian singer-songwriter, poet and novelist.

De Botton, Alain (1969); Swiss-born British philosopher and author.

Einstein, Albert (1879 — 1955); German-born physicist.

Hara, Kenya (1958); Japanese graphic designer.

Harrison, Robert Pogue (1954); Turkey-born professor of literature in America.

Hasegawa, Go (1977); Japanese architect.

Heidegger, Martin (1889 — 1976); German philosopher and a seminal thinker.

Johnson, Philip (1906 — 2005); American architect.

Kafka, Franz (1883 — 1924); German-speaking Bohemian novelist and short story writer.

Kahn, Louis Isadore (1901 — 1974); American architect.

Khayyam (1048 — 1131); Persian poet, mathematician and astronomer.

Kiarostami, Abbas (1940 — 2016); Iranian film director, screenwriter, poet, and photographer.

Kierkegaard, Soren (1813 — 1855); Danish philosopher, theologian, poet, and social critic.

Koolhaas, Rem (1945); Dutch architect.

Kundera, Milan (1929); Czech-born French writer.

Lao-Tzu (Likely 6th or 4th century BC); Ancient Chinese philosopher and writer.

Le Corbusier (1887 — 1965); Swiss-French architect, designer, painter and writer.

Lee, Bruce (1940 — 1973); Hong Kong and American actor, film director, martial artist, and philosopher.

Maeda, John (1966); American executive, designer, and technologist.

Malaparte, Curzio (1898 — 1957); Italian writer, film-maker, war correspondent and diplomat.

Martin, Agnes (1912 — 2004); Canadian-born American abstract painter.

Pallasmaa, Juhani (1936); Finnish architect.

Rumi (1207 — 1273); Persian poet and Sufi mystic.

Sana'i (1080 — 1131/41); Persian poet.

Souto de Moura, Eduardo (1952); Portuguese architect.

Stendhal (1783 — 1842); French writer.

Tsunetomo, Yamamoto (1659 — 1719); Japanese samurai and hermit.

Valéry, Paul (1871— 1945); French poet and philosopher.

Wittgenstein, Ludwig (1889 — 1951); Austrian philosopher.

Zumthor, Peter (1943); Swiss architect.

The Empty Room

Reza Aliabadi, Atelier RZLBD
Toronto, Canada
www.rzlbd.com

Edited by
Ruth Grant

Concept
Atelier RZLBD

Graphic Design
Actar Publishers

Printing and Binding
Arlequin

Paper
Coral Book

Typeface
Adriane, Futura

Publisher
Actar Publishers
New York, Barcelona
www.actar.com

Distribution
Actar D, Inc. New York, Barcelona.

New York
440 Park Avenue South, 17th Floor
New York, NY 10016, USA
T +1 2129662207
salesnewyork@actar-d.com

Barcelona
Roca i Batlle 2-4
08023 Barcelona, Spain
T +34 933 282 183
eurosales@actar-d.com

Indexing
ISBN: 978-1-948765-40-4
PCN: Library of Congress Control Number: 2019951101
Printed in Barcelona

Publication date: 2020